P9-BZE-802

FROM THE AUTHOR

—— ✴ ——

To my children:

Holly, Heather, Kent, and Carey

FROM THE ARTIST

—— ✴ ——

I would like to dedicate this book to

all the Sunday school teachers who took

the time and energy to tell me about the

most magical of all stories . . . the birth of Christ.

You are the real heroes, as heaven will

someday attest. Thank you all!

CONTENTS

GABRIEL'S MESSAGE

The Annunciation of John

WITH A HAUNTING METAPHOR, the Gospel of Luke describes Jesus' birth as "the Sunrise from on high" (1:78 NASB). The night before that sunrise had indeed been long and bleak. For four hundred years there had been no word of prophecy, no break in the darkness, no sign of the Son.

Where was the "sun of righteousness" prophesied by Malachi who would "rise with healing in [His] wings" (4:2)? And where was the one who would come first to "prepare the way for the Lord" (Isaiah 40:3)? Now the long darkness was about to end. The great plans of God Almighty, laid in eternal ages past, would begin to unfold as angels rushed to set the stage for the coming dawn.

The opening scene would be in the Temple, Herod's great Temple, described dramatically by the great Jewish historian Josephus almost two thousand years ago. The Temple lacked nothing, Josephus writes,

> that could astound either mind or eye. For, being covered on all sides with massive plates of gold, the sun was no sooner up than it radiated so fiery a flash that persons straining to look at it were compelled to avert their eyes, as from the solar rays. To approaching strangers it appeared from a distance like a snow-clad mountain; for all that was not overlaid with gold was of purest white.[1]

The Temple—this shimmering grandeur—housed the heartbeat of Jewish faith. And it was here that the curtain would begin to rise on the eternal drama.

Who would the leading players be? Unsuspecting, an elderly couple—Zechariah and Elizabeth by name—had been cast for two major parts—parts that would turn the course of history. Who were these two "unknowns" chosen for so great a role in the drama of the ages?

First there was Zechariah, an ordinary country priest. And then there was his wife, Elizabeth, who also could trace her own priestly lineage back to Aaron. "Both," the Bible tells us, "were upright in the sight of God, observing all the Lord's commands and regulations blamelessly. But they had no children, because Elizabeth was barren; and they were both well along in years" (Luke 1:5–7).

Their house enjoyed the happiness that rests upon homes where both husband and wife live a godly life. And it was a happy home—except for one thing: the couple had no children. Like childless couples at any time in history, they knew the aching disappointment, the almost unbearable stress. But in the ancient biblical world the pain was multiplied, for barrenness was considered a disgrace and even a punishment.

And now the years had taken away all hope. The spotted, worn hands of this righteous couple would never hold a child of their own.

They did not know, however, that the dawn was about to break. The occasion came on one of the two weeks each year that Zechariah was appointed to serve in the Temple. And now, chosen by an elaborate process of drawing lots, he had an added honor—to offer incense in the Holy of Holies. In an instant he was at the apex of his life! Oh, if Elizabeth could see this! What a joy he would have in telling her.

As the evening fell, the great moment approached. Zechariah stood in the heart of the gleaming Temple. Outside in the Temple courtyard the faithful worshipers were praying.

The moment arrived, and Zechariah stepped into the Holy of Holies. Before him rose the richly embroidered curtain, resplendent with cherubim woven in scarlet, blue, purple, and gold. To his left stood the table of showbread. Immediately in front of him was the golden altar of incense. To his right burned the golden candlestick. Zechariah purified the altar and waited joyously for the signal. He poured the incense on the white-hot coals, and the sacrifices went up to God, wrapped in a mixture of sweet incense and believing prayer.

Zechariah's heart soared with the curling fragrance—but suddenly his heart spasmed in divine arrest! For before him, at the right side of the incense altar, stood an angel of the Lord. Gripped with fear, Zechariah's heart began to pump in great driving drafts. Astoundingly, the angel was none other than Gabriel himself, who had last appeared 500 years before to the prophet Daniel. How fitting was the divinely intended parallel. In his former appearance to

Daniel, Gabriel revealed the future messianic times. In his present appearance to Zechariah, Gabriel signaled the *dawn* of the messianic era.

Stricken with fear, the angel comforted Zechariah. "Do not be afraid," the angel said, "your prayer has been heard." What prayer had been heard? Most likely it was Zechariah's priestly prayer for the redemption of Israel. Little did he know that the son he and Elizabeth would have would be the dawn of the answer! As Gabriel spoke, the long night of prophetic silence came to an end. After four hundred years without a word, Gabriel broke the silence with the stunning news that the messianic age was about to begin.

What was this message, borne from the presence of God Himself, on angel's wings, to an ordinary country priest? Gabriel's opening line astounded Zechariah. "Your wife Elizabeth will bear a son, and you are to give him the name John." The name John means "God has been gracious," and the logic of the name was clear. Zechariah had just prayed for God's grace to be poured out on the nation of Israel—and his prayer had been heard. A son would be born whose very name was "God has been gracious." Aged Elizabeth would experience a maternal spring; a gracious gift would come from her barren womb.

As the awesome presence of Gabriel would suggest, this would be no ordinary son. "He will be a joy and delight to you," Gabriel proclaimed, "and many will rejoice because of his birth, for he will be great in the sight of the Lord. He is never to take wine or other fermented drink, and he will be filled with the Holy Spirit even from birth. Many of the people of Israel will he bring back to the Lord their God. And he will go on before the Lord, in the spirit and power of Elijah, to turn the hearts of the fathers to their children and the disobedient to the wisdom of the righteous—to make ready a people prepared for the Lord." Their son would be none other than the one prophesied by Isaiah to "prepare the way for the Lord"—the coming Messiah.

Think now on old Zechariah. Here he stood in the heart of the Temple. The sacred ambience overwhelmed him—the light from the flickering golden candlestick, the richly embroidered hues of the cherubim on the veil, the golden altar of incense glistening in the light, the aroma of worship swirling about him. It was the grandest day of his life. Zechariah prayed for the redemption of his people. He blinked—and a supernatural being was there! There was cardiac terror. The being spoke. The promise was given. A son would be born miraculously to the aged couple, born to fulfill the final lines of the Old Testament!

The world stopped, the sunrise held, Gabriel was silent . . . and Zechariah spoke. "How can I be sure of this?" he asked in woeful disbelief. "I am an old man and my wife is well along in years."

How could he not believe! He knew the Scriptures. He knew of God's divine intervention in the births of Isaac and Samson and Samuel. He was a priest, a man of God, known for his piety and faith. He was in the very Temple of God, the Holy of Holies, and before him stood the awesome angel of the Lord.

But Zechariah disbelieved! And in his disbelief he denied the power of the gospel—namely, the power of the resurrection. For if God did not even have the power to enable Elizabeth to conceive, how could God raise Jesus' body from the tomb? Without faith in the coming "Sunrise from on high" the world would remain in darkness.

Gabriel's rebuke was swift:

> "I am Gabriel. I stand in the presence of God, and I have been sent to speak to you and to tell you this good news. And now you will be silent and not able to speak until the day this happens, because you did not believe my words, which will come true at their proper time."

Zechariah's penalty well fit the offense. His tongue, unwilling to confess belief, was struck speechless. What torture! He had so much to tell dear Elizabeth. It seemed impossible to communicate what had happened, but somehow he succeeded.

And then Elizabeth conceived! Her old body assumed the health of maternal bloom, and they were out of their minds with excitement. "The Lord has done this for me," Elizabeth rejoiced. "In these days he has shown his favor and taken away my disgrace."

The Sun would not rise until the birth of Jesus, but a pre-dawn glow had appeared on the horizon. Their faith grew and grew and grew. In six months they would host the young mother-to-be of the Son of God—and nurture her faith. They would hear her sing the *Magnificat*, and speechless Zechariah would one day sing his song of faith, the *Benedictus*.

But for us the Son *has* risen. The pre-dawn glow, prophesied by Gabriel, gave way to the full "Sunrise from on high." For us today, Jesus' words are penetratingly clear: "I am the light of the world. Whoever follows me will never walk in darkness, but will have the light of life" (John 8:12). "I tell you the truth, whoever hears my word and believes him who sent me has eternal life and will not be condemned; he has crossed over from death to life" (John 5:24). "Then they asked him, 'What must we do to do the works God requires?' Jesus answered, 'The work of God is this: to believe in the one he has sent'" (John 6:28–29).

ARTIST'S INSIGHT

———— ✳ ————

The same messenger, Gabriel, that had appeared to Daniel more than 500 years earlier now makes a surprise visit to Zechariah in the Temple. When big news was going to be announced, Gabriel was the messenger, and a visit would result in weak knees!

Again my human attempt to portray a heavenly messenger falls far short of what Gabriel must have looked like. My imagination tells me that it was spectacular beyond belief, and yet I tried to picture Gabriel so that Zechariah would be able to relate to him. I believe that God isn't interested in scaring or confusing us. Rather, His desire is to reveal Himself and His plan to us. It's possible that Gabriel appeared as a man to Zechariah. Surely any other form would have distracted from the message, which was far more important than the messenger.

I used an aggressive posture for Gabriel, trying to imagine that moment when Zechariah, who might have been praying, heard the voice of an angel. Gabriel needed to say, "Do not not be afraid . . ." I might have needed CPR! I am told that terror usually accompanied a visit from an angel. I also felt that it's possible that Gabriel appeared gradually, walking right through the altar to approach Zechariah.

The colors in the background include purple and crimson because I wanted to suggest the draping of the curtain that separated the altar of incense from the Holy of Holies. Zechariah was not allowed back there, as that was reserved for the High Priest exclusively.

The saddest part of the this scene, for me, is that it ended up with Gabriel disciplining Zechariah for unbelief. I guess that's why I left the face of Gabriel a little on the stern side. It is a reminder to me to take God at His word.

THE OVERSHADOWING

The Annunciation of Jesus

THE ANNUNCIATION is a story of singular beauty and wonder. But its beauty is especially piercing because it is true, firmly fixed in real people in an actual place in history.

The setting was in fact a shock to first-century Jews—that the angel Gabriel would ignore Judea, the heartland of God's work through the centuries, and go instead to the region of Galilee, a land of abiding contempt because of its religious impurity. Even more, that the angel would bypass the majestic city of Jerusalem for the lowly village of Nazareth.

Nazareth was a "non-place"—not even mentioned in the Old Testament or in any Jewish writings of the day. Nazareth was a shoddy, corrupt halfway stop between the port cities of Tyre and Sidon, overrun by Gentiles and Roman soldiers. Straight-talking Nathaniel, Jesus' disciple, even exclaimed, "Nazareth! Can any good thing come from there?" (John 1:46). Everybody knew Nazareth wasn't much.

Yet Gabriel skipped Judea and Jerusalem and even the Jewish Temple, the most holy place of all. By what strange divine design would the choice fall upon the humble home of Mary—which certainly wasn't much?

And in the world's eyes, Mary surely wasn't much either. She was too young to have accomplished anything—perhaps fourteen, more probably just twelve, as leading scholars conclude. A poor peasant girl, in a no-place village, she would have been illiterate, her knowledge of the Scriptures limited to what she had heard in the synagogue and committed to memory in her home.

We can only imagine how Mary felt when Gabriel appeared to her. Keep in mind Zechariah's response—being struck speechless—when Gabriel had appeared to him just six months earlier. Or recall how the great prophet Daniel fell mute too at the terrifying appearance of Gabriel some 500 years earlier. Meeting Gabriel could be intimidating—to say the least! He may well have tempered his appearance as he came to Mary or she would likely have been frightened out of her senses. But he certainly was far from conventional—no button-down collar and wingtips.

Gabriel came as an angel direct from God . . . for Mary needed to see that he indeed was an angel. Perhaps he turned up his rheostat so that he glowed like a summer firefly, or perhaps he stood with his feet just off the ground. Nothing like levitation to keep someone's attention! In the familiarity of Luke's words we almost miss the startling reality:

> In the sixth month, God sent the angel Gabriel to Nazareth, a town in Galilee,
> to a virgin pledged to be married to a man named Joseph, a descendant of
> David. The virgin's name was Mary. The angel went to her and said,
> "Greetings, you who are highly favored! The Lord is with you."

What could Mary have thought—the angel Gabriel standing before her, and then this strange greeting? What could it possibly mean? Certainly the old Douai Version's rendering, "Hail Mary full of grace," is much too strong, as both contemporary Catholic and Protestant scholars agree today. And indeed this mistaken view has given rise to an unfortunate distortion of the truth.

But before we say more, we must all agree that the Virgin Mary *is* the most blessed of women, and that "the Blessed Virgin Mary" is therefore a fitting designation. The title springs naturally from Mary's own words in her *Magnificat*: "From now on all generations will call me blessed" (Luke 1:48). Mary was the only woman out of all the billions ever to live on our planet who was chosen to carry and nurse God's Son. For that we *must* call her "blessed." The Savior was of her substance. He bore the look of her human features. Jesus' face could be seen in hers. Think of it. She is blessed indeed. Just because others have thought *too much* of her, we must not imagine that our Lord is pleased when we think *too little* of her. We rightly join with all generations to call her "blessed."

Mary's response to Gabriel's greeting reveals another of her blessed heart's qualities: "Mary was greatly troubled at his words and wondered what kind of greeting this might be."

Literally, she keep pondering the meaning of the greeting. Whatever Gabriel's glorious form was like, Mary saw beyond the angel to his greeting, searching its depths.

This is a truly remarkable picture. Young and inexperienced as she was, Mary was no flighty, shallow "young thing." She was reflective and meditative. She knew the theological grace of contemplation. She stood atop the mount of grace and meditated upon what this meant *for* her—and what it would require *from* her. In our frenetic, uncontemplative age, Mary's example has special relevance. For only those who take the time to ponder God's Word will experience the birth of the Savior in their lives.

If Mary was surprised by the initial greeting, how much more by the Annunciation itself! Gabriel's words are shocking: "But the angel said to her, 'Do not be afraid, Mary, you have found favor with God. You will be with child and give birth to a son, and you are to give him the name Jesus.'" Mary was told that she would have a baby boy, and she was commanded to name him Jesus. What a thunderbolt!

At this point Mary hardly could have understood everything. "Jesus" was a common name that meant "savior." But what did this really mean? "He will be great and will be called Son of the Most High," Gabriel continued—and the vagueness immediately evaporated. The impact must have been staggering. The child would be God's own Son! "The Lord God will give him the throne of his father David, and he will reign over the house of Jacob forever; his kingdom will never end." Gabriel was telling Mary that she would mother the long-awaited Messiah. Without a doubt Mary understood! Gabriel was reciting the messianic prophecy called the "Davidic Covenant"—the same prophetic words Mary and every devout Jew of the day had heard time and again in the synagogue readings, and longed to see fulfilled.

The meaning, in all its stupendous significance, was clear to Mary: "You are going to become *pregnant*; you are going to call your Son's name *Salvation*; He is the *Son of God*; and He will be the *Messiah*." What an earful. What an incredible heartful.

Humbly, knowingly, Mary reflected on Gabriel's words. But something didn't make sense. Her question was only logical: "How will this be since I am a virgin?" Mary wasn't disbelieving—she was simply asking for enlightenment. The question was simply biological: "God, how are You going to do this?"

Again, Mary is the spiritual model for every believer—for all who experience the Savior's birth. For the answer to Mary's question—"God, how is it possible?"—must be found by everyone who would have the birth of the Savior in their own lives.

The answer Mary received marvelously foreshadowed God's personal answer to us. "The Holy Spirit will come upon you," Gabriel explained, "and the power of the Most High will overshadow you. So the holy one to be born will be called the Son of God." Although

---

we will never fully understand this mystery, the word "overshadow" gives us the proper understanding, for it is the same word used in the Old Testament to describe God's presence in the sanctuary, and the same word used in the New Testament to describe God's presence at the Transfiguration. The Most High did overshadow Mary, and it was this transforming experience of God's presence that held her so faithful through the tumultuous days and years that followed. And whether we choose to believe it or not, the words of Gabriel describe nothing less than the virgin birth of Christ.

Remarkably, God's answer to Mary beautifully parallels the experience of everyone who has personally come to know the birth of Christ as the miraculous, life-giving work of the Holy Spirit came upon them, transforming them and bestowing life within.

Mary's encounter with Gabriel was nearly over, but before returning to the heavens, Gabriel left Mary with a sign and an unshakable promise. "Even Elizabeth your relative is going to have a child in her old age, and she who was said to be barren is in her sixth month." All of this is incredibly impossible, the modern critic would say. And as if to answer directly, Gabriel proclaimed the timeless truth that "nothing is impossible with God." God will fulfill His Word. Nothing is too hard for the All-Mighty. It is as simple as that.

Mary, of course, knew instinctively that her story would be questioned, and indeed even Joseph himself doubted. She knew that the death penalty was even prescribed for adultery in ancient Israel. But despite these daunting realities, Mary's ringing response was, "I am the Lord's servant. May it be to me as you have said." Mary's submission to God was total and absolute. Her obedience made her both the *mother* and *disciple* of the Lord.

For Luke, the theologian, Mary was the model for all who experience the birth of Christ in their lives. The answer to all our deepest needs comes in one word: *submission* to God's will. "I am the Lord's servant. May it be to me as you have said." These are the words that bring God's blessing. These are the words that bring eternal life.

In the world's eyes, Mary certainly wasn't much—a poor peasant girl in a no-place village. But she was willing to submit herself completely to the Lord. As such she reveals the eternal truth that God comes only to those who are humble and poor in spirit, who acknowledge their weakness and spiritual need, who realize they need Him—they cannot make it on their own. And to all who will give their lives to Him, He gives the gift of eternal life.

Has Christ been born in you? You need only to confess your total need to Him and give yourself to Him, and Christmas will come to your heart.

Artist's Insights

———— ✳ ————

The moment of conception is a miracle each time it happens. Certainly it's beyond the understanding of our limited minds, yet within the realm of what we know as normal. Consider Mary. A teenager confronted with the most awesome moment possible . . . the conception of One who would redeem mankind.

I have never before seen this depicted on canvas, so I certainly took a step of faith. I'm sure I didn't do justice to that incredible moment in time.

The "star" represents Christ conceived in Mary. The Scriptures refer to Christ as "the bright and morning star" (Revelation 22:16), so the symbolism of the star seems especially fitting. I put Mary in a submissive yet guarded pose, trying to signify the incredible insecurity of a meeting with holiness. Thus her arms are clenched to her chest, and her eyes are closed. It would have been too wonderful of a moment for open eyes, I have to believe.

Mary's robe and the pot in back were initially only included as "props" to date the scene. But as I began to paint her blue wrap, I was struck with the thought to put space, stars, and the heavens as symbolism—for at that moment the Eternal One became part of Mary to begin to make known the salvation of the world. The pot, on the other hand, speaks of Mary as the humble "vessel of the Lord" that would carry the eternal treasure. The shadow of a dove at her knees identifies the messenger of the miracle, the Holy Spirit.

————

ELIZABETH'S SECRET

The Visitation

THE ANGEL GABRIEL'S ANNUNCIATION declared the astounding facts of the Incarnation; the Virgin Mary's response revealed an astonishing heart. Her young heart showcased the essential characteristics of all who would experience the birth of Christ in their lives. There was her *humility*, as she was deeply conscious of her spiritual need. There was her *contemplative* soul, as she thought deeply on spiritual matters. She was profoundly *believing*, as she wondered at the miracle of her virgin conception. She was sweetly *submissive*, yielding completely to God's will. She was indeed "blessed," a living model for those who would know the life of Christ in their hearts.

What further astounds us is her tender age. As was the custom after betrothal, the bride would live with her family for a year before formally moving to the groom's home. Mary was just beyond puberty and probably hadn't even attained her full height and figure. Though it may offend the modern mind, a twelve- or thirteen-year-old girl was chosen not only to be the virgin mother of our Lord, but also to be a model of sublime faith that has challenged the greatest of saints.

We take up Mary's story with her immediate decision to visit her aged, barren relative Elizabeth. Luke reports Mary's decision with the matter-of-fact words, "At that time Mary got ready and hurried to a town in the hill country of Judah." Gabriel had just revealed to Mary that Elizabeth was pregnant and six months along. Her pregnancy was miraculous, but we must never confuse how vastly different it was from the miracle in Mary. Barren Elizabeth was not a virgin, and Zechariah was the natural father of her child. But what a surge of joy swept through Mary as she heard the shocking good news about the miracle in Elizabeth's womb, for it bore parallel testimony to God's power.

Mary made hasty arrangements with her parents (did she tell them? we do not know) and rushed the eighty to one hundred miles south, a three- or four-day journey, to the countryside of Judea. She couldn't wait to get there. There were no leisurely teenaged conversations along the way. As she hurried along, she thought long and deep of their crossed destinies. She and Elizabeth were both in miraculous pregnancies! And then she was there, unannounced, silhouetted in the old couple's doorway.

There was primal human joy in the meeting of these two expectant mothers—one in the flower of youth, the other's bloom long gone. These two were to become innocent co-conspirators, soul-sisters in the divine plan to save the lost. They would share their hearts as few ever have. Through their birthing pain, their sweat and blood, their mothering, the world would receive its ultimate blessing.

The meeting was appropriately dramatic. Luke records that Mary "entered Zechariah's home and greeted Elizabeth [and] when Elizabeth heard Mary's greeting, the baby leaped in her womb." Remarkably, the unborn baby John responded even before Elizabeth had a chance to answer Mary. In startled wonder Elizabeth replied, "As soon as the sound of your greeting reached my ears, the baby in my womb leaped for joy."

Only a mother can relate to the sensation here described. It was more than a prenatal kick or turn, but a leap, an upward vault. The same word, in fact, is used to describe skipping or leaping like that of a sheep in the field.

Why did Elizabeth's baby soar? The answer is twofold. First, she carried a prophet in her womb, and this was his first prophecy. John the Baptist's prophetic ministry was beginning three months before his birth. The Holy Spirit, already filling the unborn child, prompted his inner vault.

Second, John leaped because he was overcome with the *emotion* of joy. The exact meaning is that he "leaped with delight." What an amazing fact! John was but a six-month-old fetus, and yet he experienced emotion, joyous delight. Here is incontrovertible testimony to the pre-birth personhood of John the Baptist. John was about nine inches long and weighed about one and a half pounds. He looked like a perfect miniature newborn. His skin was translucent. He had fingerprints and toeprints. Sometimes he opened his eyes for brief periods and gazed into the liquid darkness of the womb.

Perhaps if John could have spoken, he would have quoted the Psalm, "For you created my inmost being; you knit me together in my mother's womb. I praise you because I am fearfully and wonderfully made" (Psalm 139:13–14a). As a fetus of six months, John was an emotional being. He had the capacity to be filled with the Spirit. He was so overcome that he skipped for joy. What a sobering revelation for anyone who does not believe in the sanctity of unborn babies!

As John vaulted in his mother's womb, Elizabeth too underwent an elevation of soul. The prophetic Spirit seized her, and she saluted Mary as the mother of the Lord. With a great shout she exclaimed, "Blessed are you among women, and blessed is the child you will bear! But why am I so favored, that the mother of my Lord should come to me?" How Mary's heart must have soared. For here we see that Elizabeth recognized who Jesus really was—not just a zygote in the womb of Mary, but in fact the Messiah. Elizabeth had consciously alluded to the opening line of Psalm 110, where the Messiah is referred to as "my Lord." How young Mary must have taken heart at Elizabeth's shouts. Here was one who immediately understood her secret—that she bore the Messiah in her womb!

Elizabeth then concluded her cries with a formal beatitude. With Zechariah standing by, deaf and mute because of his unbelief, Elizabeth exclaimed, "Blessed is she who has believed that what the Lord has said to her will be accomplished." Inspired by the Holy Spirit, Elizabeth's words celebrated again Mary's *faith* (in contrast to Zechariah's *unbelief*) as she submitted fully to God in order to become the mother of God's Son.

Ponder for a moment Mary's faith. To grasp it, we must understand that while *faith is belief, belief is not faith*. That is, faith is more than just intellectual belief. Faith is belief *plus* trust. Understanding this, we can discern a pattern in Mary's celebrated faith. First, she *believed* intellectually what Gabriel said—that the virgin birth was possible and would happen. Second, she *trusted* her whole life to God's promise. Third, she *rested* in God, submitting completely to His will. And fourth, out of that moment of complete rest sprang energized *action* as she immediately obeyed God's word "and hurried to a town in the hill country of Judah." Here, then, in Mary, the mother of Christ, we see the pattern of faith for everyone who would be saved. Saving faith is *belief* plus *trust*, which *rests* totally on Christ and then flames into *action*, producing a life of service. Pondering these four words can bring grace to your soul.

Do you *believe* without qualification or reservation that Jesus is God? Do you likewise believe that He died on the cross for your sins and paid for them with His blood? Do you believe that He was physically resurrected and has ascended to the right hand of God? Do you believe that you are a sinner and that your only hope is in Christ? If you do believe these things, then have you *trusted* Christ alone, relying completely on Him for your salvation? And if you have trusted Christ, have you *rested* in God alone, submitting completely to His will?

And, lastly, if you truly know the peace and rest that only God can give, has this burst forth in *active*, willing service for Christ? This alone is saving faith. If this faith is not yours already, I urge you to not let a moment pass—receive the gift of life today!

As we have moved through the account, virtually every line has added another stroke of beauty to Mary's portrait. But there is something else of immense beauty here, and that is God's care for Mary in giving her Elizabeth. Young Mary could recount Gabriel's words, but she could not be expected to fully articulate the mystery. And even if she could, who would have believed her?

But Elizabeth did! She had been prepared by her priestly husband Zechariah's dramatic experience with Gabriel, and by her own divinely wrought pregnancy. Elizabeth's profound belief in what had happened in Mary's womb—her blessing of Mary, her acknowledgment that Mary bore the Lord, her beatitude regarding Mary's faith—what a tender balm to Mary's soul! God had given young Mary a godly woman as her closest friend and confidante during this monumental time in her life.

Think of their mutuality. Both were miraculously expecting. They became sisters in experience as well as soul. Both their unborn babies had been announced by the same angel, Gabriel. Both their unborn sons had mutually fulfilling prophecies made regarding them. Imagine the women's exchange. They speculated over what the Scriptures meant. They prayed together. They talked about birth and babies. Encouragement flowed between them.

Here reality is like a dream come true. Grandmotherly Elizabeth great with child, age lines erased by pregnancy's spring, is beside the girl-virgin. Their lives were filled with expectancy, much as it is for those who first experience the new life of Christ within.

The Visitation is flesh-and-blood history about God's care for the Virgin Mary. It is about how God directed her to a community of faith, in the humble home of Zechariah and Elizabeth, where she was linked with people of mutual belief, mutual experiences, and mutual hope. The Visitation records how Mary's life within was affirmed, and how her faith was confirmed, celebrated, and strengthened. At this historic level the Visitation must first be approached. God took care of Mary!

At the same time, the Visitation offers practical insights for all who would know the birth of Christ in their lives. Here is real wisdom about real faith—that faith is belief plus trust, resting totally on the finished work of Christ, acting in a life of service for the Savior.

But the Visitation also instructs us in the necessity of the community of faith (the church) if we are to see Christ grow in our lives. Like Mary, we must fly to the church for the encouragement of those who share a *mutual faith*. There we must purposely place ourselves deep within the fellowship of those who believe the same things. Like Mary, there we

22

share the *mutual experience* of miraculous new life within. And like Mary, there our hearts are lifted up in *mutual hope and expectation*. For as the Apostle John so memorably explained, "Dear friends, now we are children of God, and what we will be has not yet been made known. But we know that when he appears, we shall be like him, for we shall see him as he is. Everyone who has this hope in him purifies himself, just as he is pure" (1 John 3:2–3).

Artist's Insights

Even though Zechariah had the benefit of the angel Gabriel's personally delivering the news of the pregnancy of of his wife, Elizabeth, the Bible records his doubt. There is no mention that Elizabeth received any such special announcement. Even Zechariah couldn't have been of much help in exclaiming the exciting news to Elizabeth since he was made dumb for his refusal to believe Gabriel. She had to go entirely on faith, just like the rest of us!

Luke 1:24 tells us that Elizabeth's faith was rewarded with her becoming pregnant with John shortly after Zechariah returned home. We are then told that Elizabeth remained in seclusion for five months after that. We are not told why, nor are we told what her thoughts were during that time. Maybe she wanted to take extra care considering her age, or maybe there were some complications we are not aware of that kept her off her feet. One thing is for sure: she was preparing for the birth of the forerunner of her Messiah. It must have consumed her every waking moment. In my painting I tried to capture one of those moments. Perhaps when some groceries were brought to the house for daily meals. A routine event. Even then the awareness of what would be written about and included in the greatest Book of all would have overshadowed her existence. I would guess she cherished every thought or reminder of it. I showed the basket of bread and fruit, significant symbols of things in the Bible, casting a shadow on the wall that takes the shape of the baby who took away her disgrace and would one day look into the eyes of Jesus as he baptized Him in the Jordan River.

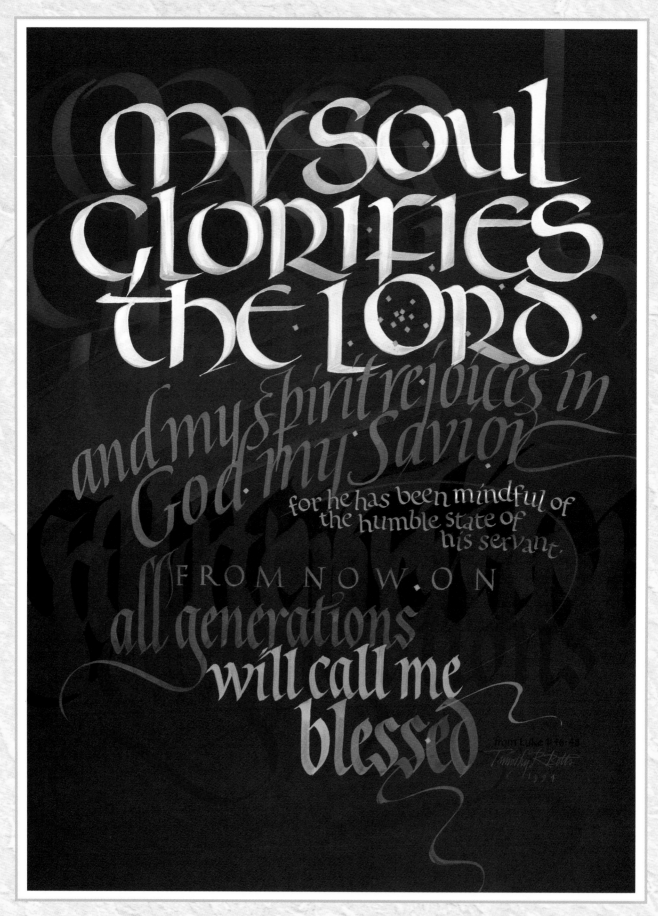

My soul glorifies the Lord and my spirit rejoices in God my Savior for he has been mindful of the humble state of his servant. FROM NOW ON all generations will call me blessed

from Luke 1:46-48

MARY'S SONG

The Magnificat

UNBORN JOHN HAD SOARED for joy in the watery darkness of Elizabeth's womb as he responded to the presence of the unborn Christ in Mary. His glad leap was prophetic of his life's mission: heralding Jesus as God's Son and Messiah. Filled with the Holy Spirit, Elizabeth responded, "Blessed are you among women, and blessed is the child you will bear!"

For a moment of stunning silence Mary and Elizabeth regarded one another. And then Mary, with majestic calm, began to sing the first song of the Incarnation. Others would follow—Zechariah's song, the angels' *Gloria*, and Simeon's hymn of praise. But this song, the *Magnificat*, is the first and the greatest.

Some have wondered how so great a song—with its majestic poetry, its rich imagery, its profound theology—could have been sung by so simple a peasant girl. The *Magnificat* is indeed a brilliantly woven tapestry of Scripture, with specific parallels to the song of Hannah, every line an allusion to the Old Testament. But those who wonder have forgotten that every young Israelite knew by heart the great Old Testament songs of Hannah and Deborah, and many Psalms of David. And could not the same Holy Spirit who overshadowed Mary at the conception of Jesus weave her words into this hallowed tapestry? The *Magnificat* was a divine/human composition, nothing less.

Lifted on the wings of the Spirit, Mary began with the unforgettable words, "My soul praises the Lord and my spirit rejoices in God my Savior." Literally, "My soul *makes great*," or as the Latin word *Magnificat* suggests, "My soul magnifies the Lord."

Of course, God cannot be made any bigger. But God can be enlarged in one's life, or in one's soul, as Mary expressed it. We "magnify" God when we catch a glimpse of His greatness. He becomes all the greater in our hearts and minds when we reflect on the wonder of His creation and Incarnation, on His death and atonement, on His resurrection and future return in power and glory. The deeper our understanding of His greatness, the greater our ability to "magnify" Him.

Knowing that she bore the Messiah, Mary had begun to think bigger and grander thoughts than ever before. "A God who could do what He did in my womb—how much more will He do in the womb of the universe!" What a wonder this is when Christ is born in *our* lives. His life courses through us, and we suddenly think greater thoughts of God than were ever possible before.

Following her opening celebration, Mary then recited her very personal reasons for her holy magnification.

Her first reason was that the Lord "has been mindful of the humble state of his servant." This is a direct allusion to the "humble state" of barren Hannah who wept bitterly before the Lord, that she might bear a child. But unlike Hannah, Mary's "humble state" was not her personal childlessness, but rather the nation of Israel's childlessness as it awaited the birth of the Messiah. Mary's "humble state" acknowledged that neither she nor her people could do anything to bring about their salvation. And like Hannah of old, Mary humbly cast herself upon God as the only one who could help.

Here we again come face to face with an essential truth of the gospel. It is only to those who realize their need, who know that they cannot save themselves, that Christ comes. Humble, helpless Mary was a nobody from a non-place. She would give birth to Jesus on the cold earth like a stranger in her homeland.

Yet it was no accident, for such has always been God's design. Soon Jesus would begin His ministry with Isaiah's prophetic words, "The Spirit of the Lord is on me, because he has anointed me to preach good news to the poor" (quoting 61:1). Likewise, the startling words of the Sermon on the Mount were, "Blessed are the poor in spirit, for theirs is the kingdom of heaven. Blessed are those who mourn, for they will be comforted. Blessed are the meek, for they will inherit the earth" (Matthew 5:3–5). The eternal truth is, "The Lord is close to the brokenhearted and saves those who are crushed in spirit" (Psalm 34:18).

May this not be wasted on us! Christ comes only to the humble in spirit. He does not come to the mechanized Christmas windows at the shopping mall. He does not appear on television's Christmas specials. He does not warm to the Boston Pops cassette of Christmas favorites.

Is this a negative teaching? Not at all! Unlike riches and power, the grace of humility is available to us all—specifically to the "brokenhearted" and to those who are "crushed in spirit." The gift is for all who know their "humble state"!

Mary's second reason for magnifying the Lord came in the words, "From now on all generations will call me blessed." At first glance it may seem that Mary was lifting up herself. But the focus here is not upon Mary, but upon what God is going to do for "all generations." "From now on" is literally, *"For behold!"* (*"Look!"*)—an exclamation of surprise. Mary was filled with wonder that all future generations would pronounce beatitudes over her name, until the end of the world. What a mind-boggling truth was revealed to this young teenager by the Holy Spirit.

But it is true. She was and is "blessed." There were actually times when Mary could be seen in God's Son—in the line of His smile, in the mold of His forehead, in His walk, His accent, His expressions. Mary must always be "blessed."

But hear this: If we are Christians, if Jesus is truly born in us, we too will be called blessed far beyond earth's history. Jesus Himself tells us, "Then the King will say to those on his right, 'Come, you who are blessed by my Father; take your inheritance, the kingdom prepared for you since the creation of the world'" (Matthew 25:34). And again, "Blessed and holy are those who have part in the first resurrection" (Revelation 20:6).

And if this is not enough, we will even bear a resemblance to Jesus. As the Apostle John writes, "Dear friends, now we are children of God, and . . . we know that when he appears, we shall be like him" (1 John 3:2). But the remarkable truth here is not that we will physically resemble the Lord, but that we will have His character, His purity, the heart of Christ. This is the ultimate blessedness! Let us, too, magnify the Lord!

✳ ✳ ✳

In the second half of the *Magnificat*, Mary moved from giving her *personal* reasons for magnifying the Lord to giving *prophetic* reasons. The movement was quite natural—like the common experience of riding a ship up to a wave's crest. You begin down in the dark trough, but as the wave swells, you ride upward to its bright crest. From there you can look across the surrounding waves to the rimming horizon and intermittent islands and distant landfall.

Mary's soul was carried upward as she sang of her *personal* reasons. Then, from the crest of the wave, her soul reached toward the horizons of the world as she sang of the *prophetic* reasons for magnifying the Lord. The change from personal to prophetic was quite natural, because God's dealings with individual souls are according to the same principles as those which guide His dealings with the world. In the microcosm of her own life Mary saw how God would deal with the whole world—and she sang in praise of those great reasons.

In the second half of the *Magnificat*, we also see that Mary began to prophesy using the past tense: "he has performed," "he has scattered," "he has brought down," "he has lifted up." If this is prophecy, we might ask, why did Mary speak in the past tense, as if God had already accomplished all of these things? Here Mary stood in the stream of the great prophets of old. Like Isaiah and Jeremiah and Ezekiel, Mary's prophetic words were put in the past tense to emphasize two time- less truths—first, that God had indeed already done these things in past history, but also that what God will do in the future is so certain that we may properly speak of it as already having been accomplished. Thus Mary brought together history and prophecy: what God had done in the past was irrefutable evidence for what He would do in the future through the work of the Son.

What are the prophetic truths that Mary proclaimed here through the inspiration of the Holy Spirit?

First, there was the great social/moral reversal that the Messiah-Son would bring to life. Mary proclaimed that God "has scattered those who are proud. . . . He has brought down rulers from their thrones." God does indeed bring down the strutting proud, the arrogant, the conceited. Looking back in history, we see how God destroyed arrogant Pharaoh and his defiant armies; how he crushed the pride of Nebuchadnezzar, reducing him to a beast of the field until that monarch turned to God in abject humility; how He struck down Belshazzar on the very night of his strutting pride, destroying the Babylonian empire in a single day.

But the promises of the past will be fulfilled with equal certainty in the future. We see glimpses of the great social/moral reversal in the subsequent annals of history. Prideful Herod Agrippa stood in his splendid royal robes enjoying the blasphemous praise of an admiring audience. "This is the voice of a god, not of a man," they said. But Luke tells us, "Immediately, because Herod did not give praise to God, an angel of the Lord struck him down, and he was eaten by worms and died" (Acts 12:23). Napoleon had his proud Austerlitz, but then came Russia and Waterloo. Hitler launched his *Anschluss*, but a few years later D-Day came. And today the grand sculptured heads of Lenin and Stalin lie in junkyards awaiting the torch. Our days echo the crash of falling thrones.

But most of all, Mary sang of the final reversal and reckoning that awaits those who proudly reject the work of Christ. "He has scattered those who are proud in their inmost thoughts," Mary sang. Twice the New Testament repeats the theme, "God opposes the proud but gives grace to the humble" (James 4:6; 1 Peter 5:5). Those who are "proud in their inmost thoughts"—because of health or education or privilege or a feeling of moral superiority—are in for a rude awakening. And if they do not repent and turn to God, their fate is an accomplished fact—it has already been sealed. This great truth is a done deal that will be fully played out in the final judgment.

The gospel lifts up the humble and casts down the proud. Life is not as it appears. Spiritually, *down is up, and up is down!* Jesus Himself is the great example. Because of His willing humiliation in the Incarnation and on the cross, He has been lifted above every power and throne. As the Apostle Paul wrote,

> Therefore God exalted him to the highest place and gave him the name that is above every name, that at the name of Jesus every knee should bow, in heaven and on earth and under the earth, and every tongue confess that Jesus Christ is Lord, to the glory of God the Father. (Philippians 2:9–11)

But Mary also sang of material/spiritual reversal: "He has filled the hungry with good things but has sent the rich away empty." Here is a rock-solid principle. Those in physical/material need are typically more inclined to sense their spiritual need than the rich and satisfied. As the Psalms so often teach, spiritual hunger is the prescription for spiritual health: "As the deer pants for streams of water, so my soul pants for you, O God. My soul thirsts for God, for the living God" (Psalm 42:1–2); "My soul faints with longing for your salvation" (Psalm 119:81).

By contrast we are reminded of the rich young ruler who had everything he thought he needed and missed the only thing he really needed; or the parable of the poor man and Lazarus, who was blinded by his abundance until it was too late. As Christians we see that our spiritual hunger is in fact a blessed state. Paradoxically it works like this: when we hunger spiritually, we are filled and supremely satisfied. But our satisfaction then makes way for a deeper spiritual hunger, and a further filling and blessed satisfaction. And so it goes on in sublime paradox—as we become ever fuller in Christ.

This is the message of the *Magnificat*; this is the message of Christmas. Christ came to the hungry—to young Mary, to aged Simeon and Anna, to fishermen, tax collectors—to the desperately hungry who were sent away eternally full. "Blessed are those who [continually] hunger and thirst for righteousness, for they will be filled" (Matthew 5:6). The divine reward is complete satisfaction. As so many Scriptures attest: "Whoever drinks the water I give him will never thirst. Indeed, the water I give him will become in him a spring of water welling up to eternal life" (John 4:14). "I am the bread of life. He who comes to me will never go hungry" (John 6:35). And as Mary affirmed—for the past, present, and eternal future—"He has filled the hungry with good things."

God is seeking hearts like Mary's—children who magnify Him in their hearts and souls. Theirs is the Gift of Christmas—Christ the Savior, born within—eternal life forevermore.

———

THE FORERUNNER

The Birth of JOHN

ARY STAYED WITH ELIZABETH for the remaining three months of the old woman's pregnancy. Most likely she was present at the birth of John to witness this event of singular joy. Elizabeth, in the autumn of life, experienced the spring rhythm of labor and birth. And in a sublimely poignant moment, loving hands (perhaps the hands of the Virgin) placed her son into her arms. No doubt godly Elizabeth recalled the joy and laughter of another aged mother, Sarah, at the birth of Isaac. Sarah laughed, Abraham laughed, and joy filled the tents of his people. Now Elizabeth too laughed aloud and wept for joy. Zechariah laughed silently as tears coursed down his gray beard. Laughter, mixed with their son's cries, rang across the hillsides of Judea.

As Luke relates, "Her neighbors and relatives heard that the Lord had shown her great mercy, and they shared the joy." At first they were incredulous; they didn't even know Elizabeth was pregnant. The secret had been well kept by mute Zechariah and the Virgin. But their initial skepticism disappeared when they came and saw for themselves radiant Elizabeth calmly nursing her son.

On the eighth day after his birth, Zechariah and Elizabeth prepared for the covenant rite of circumcision. All the neighbors and relatives came in festive spirit for the happy occasion. A great crowd certainly was there; none would miss this amazing event for the firstborn of their aged friend and relative! The circumcision would mark the boy with the sign of the

31

covenant and set him apart for the blessings promised to God's people. The fulfillment of this rite on the eighth day gave him the impeccable Jewish credentials so necessary for the Messiah's forerunner.

What was his name to be? The relatives all agreed that certainly he must be called Zechariah after his father. But immediately his mother spoke up. "No! He is to be called John." Unaware of the divinely appointed name, the relatives persisted. "They said to her, 'There is no one among your relatives who has that name.' Then they made signs to his father, to find out what he would like to name the child. He asked for a writing tablet, and to everyone's astonishment he wrote, 'His name is John.'"

It is difficult for us to appreciate what a jolt this was to the family. Jewish children were *always* named after someone in the family. The double insistence of the aged couple was truly shocking. But John's divinely appointed name was intended to stir their spiritual imaginations. "John"—literally, "The Lord has given grace"—was the fitting title for the child who would be the Savior's forerunner. But there is more here, for in giving the child a name of God's own choosing, God indicated that John's mission and power came from outside the natural order.

No sooner had Zechariah finished writing the last letter of his son's name than "Immediately his mouth was opened and his tongue was loosed, and he began to speak, praising God." His initial doubt had given way to faith, and faith in turn to obedience. As he doggedly insisted that his son should be named John, his obedience set his tongue loose in a song of praise. Again the neighbors and relatives were jolted. Think of the spiritual voltage here! Zechariah had endured nine months of speechless frustration. Now all the pent-up frustration poured out in loud, emotional praise upon praise.

What a dramatic scene this was. "The neighbors were all filled with awe," Luke says, "and throughout the hill country of Judea people were talking about all these things." They sensed God was at work, and exhilarating fear coursed through their souls. "Everyone who heard this wondered about it, asking, 'What then is this child going to be?' For the Lord's hand was with him."

* * *

The night before the sunrise of Jesus' birth had, indeed, been long and bleak. According to the Scriptures the people had been "living in darkness and in the shadow of death"—like a caravan lost in a desert night, fearing for life. The faithful remnant, of course, knew that the messianic sunrise would come, for the prophet Malachi had memorably promised, "The sun of righteousness will rise with healing in its wings. And you will go out and leap like calves released from the stall" (4:2).

And now there had come the first flashes of light, prefiguring the dawn that would soon appear: Gabriel's annunciation of John to Zechariah; Gabriel's annunciation of Jesus to Mary;

the meeting of the two pregnant mothers and Elizabeth's joyful prophecy; Mary's magnificent song; the birth of John the Baptist. These momentary flashes were signs assuring that the steady rays of messianic sunlight would soon shine from the horizon. Now, after the birth of John, a faint glow was almost perceptible.

Old Zechariah, nine months speechless because of unbelief, had now responded in faithful obedience. His tongue was loosed—and he gave *the final song before the sunrise*. Zechariah stood as the prophetic mouthpiece of God; his words were God's words. As with Mary's own magnificent song, his too was filled with Scripture. The hymn is traditionally called the *Benedictus* because the opening words—"Praise be to the Lord, the God of Israel"—were rendered in the Latin Vulgate Bible with the words, *"Benedictus Dominus Deus Israel."* The title is fitting indeed, for this song of praise and benediction unfolded the covenant plan of God to bring salvation to the world through His coming Son.

"Zechariah," Luke records, "was filled with the Holy Spirit and prophesied":

> "'Praise be to the Lord, the God of Israel, because he has come and redeemed his people. He has raised up a horn of salvation for us in the house of his servant David (as he said through his holy prophets of long ago), salvation from our enemies and from the hand of all who hate us—to show mercy to our fathers and to remember his holy covenant, the oath he swore to our father Abraham: to rescue us from the hand of our enemies, and to enable us to serve him without fear in holiness and righteousness before him all our days.'"

This song before the sunrise was an ecstatic chain of praise from beginning to end. In this first half Zechariah recounted God's eternal covenants to David and Abraham. The immediate context of God's promise to David was that Solomon would succeed him on the throne. But the final fulfillment was to come in the future, when God would place His own Son on the Davidic throne to rule over His eternal Kingdom forever. The mighty "horn of salvation" is the King of Kings and Lord of Lords who redeems us and delivers us from our sins.

Today this mighty "horn of salvation" is able "to save completely those who come to God through him" (Hebrews 7:25). Whoever we are, whatever we have done, no matter how heinous our sin—whether it is murder, infidelity, perversion, betrayal, embezzlement, lying, jealousy, hateful gossip, or whatever—Christ, the "horn of salvation," can save us completely and eternally. This is the wonder of the gospel—"it is the power of God for the salvation of everyone who believes" (Romans 1:16).

Similarly, Zechariah harkened back even further to God's covenant promise to Abraham.

As the Apostle Paul wrote, Abraham "believed God, and it was credited to him as righteousness . . . [and all] those who believe are children of Abraham" (Galatians 3:6–7). Moreover, "If [we] belong to Christ, then [we] are Abraham's seed, and heirs according to the promise" (3:29). Thus we may rest in the prophetic promises of Zechariah's song: God will "enable us to serve him without fear in holiness and righteousness before him all our days."

As Zechariah came to the middle of his song, we can well imagine that his eyes fell to his newborn son, and he sang of his part in the new day: "And you, my child, will be called a prophet of the Most High; for you will go on before the Lord to prepare the way for him, to give his people the knowledge of salvation through the forgiveness of their sins" (vv. 76–77).

We cannot overdraw Zechariah's emotion here. There had been no prophet among the Jews for four centuries. Zechariah had just recovered his voice, and he was prophesying. Now, his baby boy was the brief focus of divine revelation. His words were not calm utterances. They came in a halting, tremulous voice as he struggled to gain composure. His son would "give his people the knowledge of salvation." This would not be theoretical knowledge but *personal* knowledge—the inward experience of salvation as the result of a divine gift.

But more than this, the salvation that John would preach would consist of "the forgiveness of their sins." In this, John's ministry anticipated the work of the coming sunrise. We see this in Jesus' very name as given by the angel: "She will give birth to a son, and you [Joseph] are to give him the name Jesus, because he will save his people from their sins" (Matthew 1:21). Likewise, Jesus said of His own blood, "This is my blood of the covenant, which is poured out for many for the forgiveness of sins" (Matthew 26:28). Thus we have the assurance, "If we confess our sins, he is faithful and just and will forgive us our sins and purify us from all unrighteousness" (1 John 1:9).

What incredible things Zechariah sang regarding his son! True "knowledge of salvation" and "the forgiveness of sins" would come from his ministry. This is what the gospel offers: authentic forgiveness—the only real forgiveness of sins in the universe. Those who have experienced it can testify that there is nothing like it. It is complete and penetrates to the depth of our being.

Zechariah ended his song with praise for the imminent rising of the sun: "because of the tender mercy of our God, by which the rising sun will come to us from heaven to shine on those living in darkness and in the shadow of death, to guide our feet into the path of peace" (vv. 78–79).

The nation of Israel was portrayed here as a caravan that had lost its way and had been overtaken by night. They were stranded in utter darkness, in a black, howling expanse. The sky was lowering; there was no starlight. They were helpless, just as Isaiah described it: "people walking in darkness . . . living in the land of the shadow of death" (9:2).

———

But then—a faint change was seen in the east. The sky was no longer black but cobalt. A hint of light, a wisp of color, and the cobalt turned to royal blue. A long line of pink rimmed the horizon. "The rising sun will come to us from heaven"!

Here was the fulfillment of Malachi's prophecy: "for you who revere my name, the sun of righteousness will rise with healing in its wings. And you will go out and leap like calves released from the stall" (4:2). Jesus is "the morning star" who rises in our hearts (2 Peter 1:19). He is "the Root and the Offspring of David, and the bright Morning Star" (Revelation 22:16). Of Himself Jesus said, "I am the light of the world. Whoever follows me will never walk in darkness, but will have the light of life" (John 8:12).

When Jesus rises in our lives, gone is "the shadow of death." We pass from death to life. He guides "our feet into the path of peace." He gives His promise, "Peace I leave with you; my peace I give you" (John 14:27). And we "leap like calves released from the stall"—heels in the air, free and complete!

ARTIST'S INSIGHTS

John, in most of our minds, is exceptionally important. In Scripture he is compared to Elijah. Jesus said, "Among those born of women there has not risen anyone greater . . ." (Matthew 11:11, NIV). Certainly his role as the forerunner of the Messiah is the greatest title one could hold. What an honor! There is, however, a part of me that wonders how Zechariah and Elizabeth viewed John. He was their baby boy. Did they know that his lot would be to spend his future in the desert, with hardly a traditional lifestyle? To one day succumb to the sword of an evil ruler surely could not have been their hope for him. Never does true greatness collide more dramatically with human thinking than in this case. The singing group 4-Him has a song that says, "I want to be a man you would write about 1,000 years from now." That's John.

I tried to portray John's beginning as a baby like all of us, with his future in the distance. The lightning symbolizes the tumultuous life he would experience. The hand intersecting the baby would at first be thought as the tender hand of old Zechariah about to gently alight on his boy. I made it larger and more "heavenly" to make a bigger statement, though. The hand of God was on John from the beginning. John was set apart for service to God from conception. (Psalm 4:3 tells us we are, too. What an encouragement!) If God has a job for our children, will we entrust them to God? It looks like Zechariah wasn't that faithless after all!

THE GIFT

FROM GROUND LEVEL, Joseph and Mary were insignificant nobodies from a noth-ing town. They were peasants. They were poor, uneducated, of no account. Joseph and Mary capsulized the mystery of grace—because the King does not come to the proud and powerful, but to the poor and powerless. As happens so often in life, things were not as they seemed to the world around, because humble Mary and Joseph were the father and mother of the King of Kings.

They appeared to be helpless pawns caught in the movements of secular history. But every move was being made by the hand of God. The Messiah *had* to be born in tiny, insignif-icant Bethlehem! As the virgin traveled, she bore under her steady beating heart, hidden from the world, the busy thumping heart of God.

> *The Creator had woven Himself*
> *a robe of virgin*
> *flesh.²*

The baby Mary carried was not a Caesar, a man who would claim to be a god, but a far greater wonder—God who had become a man!

The journey left Mary increasingly weary as she trod those dusty miles to the south. And when she and Joseph arrived in Bethlehem they were exhausted—especially Mary. And then the pains began. Perhaps at first young Mary wasn't sure and didn't say anything to Joseph. But then, when there was no doubt that it was the real thing, she informed him—probably with tears. She was just a girl of thirteen or fourteen years.

We are all familiar with the haunting simplicity of Luke's description of the birth: "While they were there, the time came for the baby to be born, and she gave birth to her firstborn, a son."

In Bethlehem the accommodations for travelers were primitive. The eastern inn was the crudest of arrangements. Typically it was a series of stalls built on the inside of an enclosure and opening onto the common yard where the animals were kept. All the innkeeper provided was fodder for the animals and a fire to cook on. On that cold day when the expectant parents arrived, nothing at all was available, not even one of those crude stalls. And despite the urgency no one would make room for them. So it was probably in the common courtyard where the travelers' animals were tethered that Mary gave birth to Jesus—with only Joseph attending.

Joseph must have wept, as well as Mary. Mary's pain, the stinking barnyard, their poverty, the indifference, the humiliation, the sense of utter helplessness, the shame of not being able to provide for young Mary on the night of her travail—it would make a man either curse or cry.

If we imagine that it was into a freshly swept, County Fair stable that Jesus was born, we miss the whole point. It was wretched—scandalous! There was sweat and pain and blood and cries as Mary reached to the stars for help. The earth was cold and hard. The smell of birth was mixed into a wretched bouquet with the stench of manure and acrid straw. Trembling carpenter's hands, clumsy with fear, grasped God's Son slippery with blood—the baby's limbs waving helplessly as if falling through space—his face grimacing as he gasped the cold and his cry pierced the night.

> *My mother groaned, my father wept.*
> *Into the dangerous world I leapt.*[3]

It was a leap down—as if the Son of God rose from his splendor, stood poised at the rim of the universe, and dove headlong, speeding through the stars over the Milky Way to earth's galaxy, finally past Arcturus, where he plunged into a huddle of animals. Nothing could be lower.

Luke finishes the picture: "She wrapped him in strips of cloth and placed him in a manger, because there was no room for them in the inn." Mary counted his fingers. She and Joseph wiped him clean as best they could by firelight, and Mary wrapped each of his little round, steaming arms and legs with strips of cloth—mummy-like. No one helped her. She laid him in a feeding trough.

It was low. No child born into the world that day seemed to have lower prospects. The Son of God was born into the world not as a prince but as a pauper. We must never forget that this is where Christianity began—and where it always begins. It begins with a sense of need, a graced sense of one's insufficiency. Christ comes to the needy. Ultimately, he is born in those who are "poor in spirit."

The story moves quickly as Christ's birth is announced. Shepherds were the first to hear. "And there were shepherds living out in the fields nearby, keeping watch over their flocks at night. An angel of the Lord appeared to them, and the glory of the Lord shone around them, and they were terrified." The shepherds on that wintry night were naturally huddled close to their fire, while above, the icy constellations swept by. Suddenly, as if a star burst, glory dazzled the night, and an honored angel stepped forth as the shepherds recoiled in great fear—despite his reassuring words.

That the message came to shepherds first, and not to the high and mighty, once again brings us to the refrain that God comes to the needy, the "poor in spirit." Shepherds were despised by the "good," respectable people of that day. They were regarded as thieves. The only ones lower than shepherds, at this particular time in Jewish history, were lepers.

God wants us to get it straight: He comes to those who sense their need. He does not come to the self-sufficient. Christmas is for those who need Jesus! Whatever our situation, He can deliver us. The angel said the "good news" was for "all the people." Whoever you are, He can deliver you. "Because Jesus lives forever . . . he is able to save completely those who come to God through him, because he always lives to intercede for them" (Hebrews 7:24–25). Listen to the angel's words, again, slowly: "Do not be afraid. I bring you good news of great joy that will be for all the people. Today in the town of David a Savior has been born to you; he is Christ the Lord."

Now see what happens. "Suddenly a great company of the heavenly host appeared with the angel, praising God and saying, 'Glory to God in the highest, and on earth peace to men on whom his favor rests.'" Here we need a little Christmas imagination. Perhaps there was a flash and suddenly the bewildered shepherds were surrounded by angels.

Note well that it says that it was a "great company"—beyond count. I think that *every* angel was there because this was the most amazing and greatest event that had ever happened in the universe. I think they stretched from horizon to horizon, obscuring the winter constellations. I like to imagine that they radiated gold, pink, electric blue, hyacinth, and ultraviolet—and that some were sparkling. And then, when they lifted their voices to God, it was in cosmic stereo!

How we all would like to have been there—to be a fly on the ear of one of the shepherds' sheep. But hear this: though the choir in Heaven did it, we on earth have a part, *and it is the best part, because we are children of grace*. God became a *man*, not an angel. God redeemed *us*, not angels. Ours is the best part, and we will sing it for eternity!

The angels departed, the glory that lit the countryside faded, the constellations reappeared, and the shepherds were alone. They allowed no grass to grow under their feet. They took off running, leaping the low Judean fences, and entered the enclosure wide-eyed and panting. They searched the stalls and quickly found the new mother and her Babe out in the open among the animals. Immediately they began to announce the good news, telling all who would listen about the angels and the baby. When they left, they continued glorifying and praising God for all they had experienced.

This Christmas it is not enough to hear about Jesus. It is not enough to come peek in the manger and say, "Oh, how nice. What a lovely scene. It gives me such good feelings." The truth is, even if Christ were born in Bethlehem a thousand times and not in you, you would be eternally lost. The Christ who was born into the world must be born in your heart.

Christmas sentiment without the living Christ is a yellow brick road to darkness. That is the terrifying thing about all the Christmas glitz—that Christmas can be buried by materialism and sentiment and people will not even know it or care.

He really did come into the world; and because of this, he really can come into your heart. This Christmas, let us lay our lives before Him and receive the gift.

In this world of sin,
Where meek souls will
receive him still
The dear Christ enters in.[4]

The Nativity has been painted by countless artists through the ages. Mostly, I would guess they portray a version that is closer to what we want to think than what actually might have been. But no matter what the outward circumstances were, no one who was there could have been aware of the profound meaning of that night, or of that Baby—nobody, except perhaps the unseen visitors who stood in awesome vigil for the Baby they already had known as the "King of Kings and Lord of Lords."

In portraying an angel at the moment when this realization takes place, I can only imagine the thoughts that seared his mind. Surely this night represented the highest joy possible. But for whom? Isaiah prophesied hundreds of years earlier that Christ would be "disfigured beyond that of any man and his form marred beyond human likeness" (Isaiah 52:14). Read on in that book and you will begin to see the awesome love of God in that Baby. For He was born crucified.

It occurs to me that nearly everyone loves the Christmas story with the Baby, but few are willing to bow to the man on the cross. Christ was not born for Christmas, He was born for Easter! That's why I put a lamb at the foot of the trough. As John would one day exclaim, "Look, the Lamb of God, who takes away the sin of the world!" (John 1:29).

If we could get a true glimpse of Christmas, we would probably have to swallow hard and take a deep breath at the reality of what Christ started on that starry night. It is summed up in Hebrews 12:2—"Let us fix our eyes on Jesus, the author and perfecter of our faith, who for the joy set before him endured the cross, scorning its shame, and sat down at the right hand of the throne of God." Something to remember the next time we sing "Silent Night."

SIMEON'S MOMENT

IT HAD BEEN FORTY DAYS since Mary felt the pains of birth and first held her little Son against her breast. Now Joseph and Mary had just finished retracing their journey, this time traveling as three to Jerusalem. But why would they travel again so soon and with their little one not yet six weeks old? As Dr. Luke explains:

> When the time of their purification according to the Law of Moses had been completed, Joseph and Mary took him to Jerusalem to present him to the Lord (as it is written in the Law of the Lord, "Every firstborn male is to be consecrated to the Lord"), and to offer a sacrifice in keeping with what is said in the Law of the Lord.

Luke's words are pregnant with meaning. Here the Giver of the Law is fulfilling the Law. Here is the newborn Son being presented to the Father whose loving embrace He had known for all eternity. Here is a sacrifice being offered for the one who would Himself become the sacrifice for all the world.

How Joseph and Mary must have retraced their memories as they retraced their steps that day on the way to Jerusalem. Was there still a hint of fear as Mary recalled Gabriel's astounding words?—"Do not be afraid, Mary, you have found favor with God. You will be with child and give birth to a son."

Surely the wonder of the recent weeks burned bright in their thoughts and words as they made their way to Jerusalem—how the skies had blazed with a myriad of angels; how the shepherds had run, leaping the low pasture fences, shouting the news, "The Savior has been born!"

As they reflected on those days since the first light of Christmas morn, surely they returned often to their little Son's name. "You are to give him the name Jesus," Gabriel had announced to Mary. And Gabriel repeated the identical words to Joseph, "You are to give him the name Jesus." And so it was, as Luke records, that "On the eighth day, when it was time to circumcise him, he was named Jesus."

It was important that Christ be circumcised. Circumcision was commanded for all males who would be a part of Abraham's household. Without it He would not be identified with His people, even though he was of pure Hebrew blood.

But the matter of greatest significance was his name—Jesus—officially given at His circumcision. Certainly Mary and Joseph had often discussed his name, both before his birth and during the weeks that followed. But when the time for circumcision came and Joseph uttered the divinely given name, the sense of the moment must have overwhelmed them. Their child was to be called "*Jesus*"—literally, "Jehovah is salvation." "This child, our baby, is salvation!" What a birth memory for them to cherish!

✳ ✳ ✳

Forty days . . . "the time of their purification" . . . the time "to present him to the Lord" in the Temple in Jerusalem. As they approached the magnificent Temple, it rose before them in stunning splendor. The massive columns, the intricate patterns, the dazzling gold everywhere they looked—it was almost too much for the senses to take in.

With the Temple towering before them, how small they must have felt approaching the altar to offer their sacrifice, "a pair of doves or two young pigeons." It was a poor woman's offering. We know this because the book of Leviticus requires a yearling lamb—except, as Moses wrote, "If she cannot afford a lamb, she is to bring two doves or two young pigeons, one for a burnt offering and the other for a sin offering" (12:8). The humble bird-offering of Mary and Joseph was a public declaration of their poverty. And so we are reminded again— it is the persistent refrain of Christ's birth—that God does not come to the self-sufficient, but to those of humble state who hunger and thirst for the gift of the Savior.

But before Mary and Joseph could even approach the altar, they themselves were approached by a man with outstretched arms, his face radiant with joy and expectation. What a welcome they must have received! The words of Scripture tell it best:

> Now there was a man in Jerusalem called Simeon, who was righteous and devout. He was waiting for the consolation of Israel, and the Holy Spirit was upon him. It had been revealed to him by the Holy Spirit that he would not die before he had seen the Lord's Christ. Moved by the Spirit, he went into the temple courts. When the parents brought in the child Jesus to do for him what the custom of the Law required, Simeon took him in his arms . . .

Here is something more to put in our treasury of Christmas memories. We see the stooped profile of Simeon, advanced in years, with age-spotted hands but a soul that was brimming with life! "Righteous and devout," Simeon knew the only hope was the mercy and grace of God. He longed for righteousness; he thirsted for consolation. How long had he been waiting? Days? Months? Years? We cannot know. But we can imagine his quiet assurance as daily he came to the Temple looking. "Is this the one? There's a likely couple! Maybe this is it!"

And then on that great day, the Holy Spirit prompted him. "Moved by the Spirit," Simeon accosted Mary and Joseph—and with trembling arms lifted the fat, dimpled baby from the startled virgin. And for a moment the world ceased to turn as he received God Incarnate into his quaking hands. He looked at Jesus . . . and looked . . . and looked again. And his heart soared in prophetic song:

> "Sovereign Lord, as you have promised, you now dismiss your servant in peace. For my eyes have seen your salvation, which you have prepared in the sight of all people, a light for revelation to the Gentiles and for glory to your people Israel."

With the baby in his arms, in the aura of God's presence, Simeon experienced a profound soul-peace. And well he should, for he held the "prince of peace." The "sun of righteousness" had come; the day of redemption had dawned. With his own eyes Simeon had seen the salvation of the Lord.

Simeon was indeed overcome with peace. He held the Gift in his hands and embraced the Gift with his soul. But the astonishing truth of Simeon's song is that salvation is for *all* who will themselves embrace the Savior. Like Simeon, all we have to do is take Him as Lord into our arms.

Do we see the amazing significance of this moment? It was not lost on Joseph and Mary, for "The child's father and mother marveled at what was said about him." May we too come to profound amazement—and thus hold every word close to our heart.

But from the lofty heights of ecstasy, Simeon quickly brings us back to the reality of our need for the Savior and what the work of our salvation would mean. "This child is destined," Simeon proclaims, "to cause the falling and rising of many in Israel, and to be a sign that will be spoken against, so that the thoughts of many hearts will be revealed."

"To cause the falling and rising"—unwelcome though these words sound to the world today, again we hear the persistent theme of Christmas. For only when we fall before the Savior in humiliation and poverty of spirit will we rise to new life in Christ. What a message of hope! For the grace of humility, unlike riches or power, is available to all. "The Lord is close to the brokenhearted and saves those who are crushed in spirit," the psalmist says. Like Mary, we can rejoice in our "humble state," for Christ comes to us in our greatest need.

But what of Simeon's closing words? "A sword will pierce your own soul too." Mary would indeed know the blessedness of the *Magnificat*, but she would also know the sorrow foretold by Simeon. There would be the flight into Egypt. Her Son would be despised and rejected. There would be His passion. A sword would pierce the Savior's side as He would bear the sins of the world on the cross. But a sword would also pierce His mother's soul. How costly was the Gift God gave. How great His love for us. "For God so loved the world that he gave his one and only Son, that whoever believes in him shall not perish but have eternal life" (John 3:16).

* * *

As we too retrace the memories of that first Christmas, we discover anew the "sun of righteousness" who comes with healing in [His] wings." What a plunging leap He took—as if the Son of God rose from His heavenly splendor, stood poised on the rim of the universe, and dove headlong through the galaxies to be born of a simple peasant girl in a crude and humble place. But here we see the wonder of Christmas! The Gift comes only to those who humbly know their need, "who hunger and thirst for righteousness."

Do you know your need for the Savior? Will you then receive the Gift? To all who will He promises, "I am the resurrection and the life. He who believes in me will live, even though he dies; and whoever lives and believes in me will never die" (John 11:25–26).

Here is the Gift of Christmas—Christ the Savior born in our hearts—eternal life forevermore.

Imagine that moment! It has to rank at the top of any Christian's list of dreams—to hold the very Son of God in your arms and understanding His purpose for coming. This is what Simeon had been promised, and here He is. It was the final exclamation point to fulfill his heart's desire.

Because of what his eyes saw and his hands felt, Simeon was content, ready to leave and go be with his God. We can only guess (I like to do that at times) what must have raced through Simeon's mind at that moment. He didn't have long to hold Him, but long enough to realize that Messiah had come.

In this painting I tried to let Simeon's face tell the story. Ecstasy. I have a feeling Simeon clutched that baby like none other. He knew that he held the "light" of the world, which I symbolized by the star emanating from the baby. Intertwined through them both, I put a map of the world with its obvious symbolism that Christ came to impact the whole world, and not just the Jews as most of the people would have concluded. Simeon knew. I purposely made the map showing the world as we know it today. Those lands, like North and South America, as well as others, were not even known to Simeon's world, but God knew all along that we would need a Savior. Simeon's tear was put in to reflect deep joy. But the more I contemplated it, the more I realized it could symbolize that Simeon also might have known that this Baby was born to be crucified. That was why He came.

NOTES

———— ✳ ————

1. Josephus, *War*, V.5.3.
2. Paraphrased from *Pestle on the Incarnation* (1584-1654).
3. Michael Mason, editor, *William Blake*, The Oxford Authors Series, "Infant Sorrow," from "Songs of Innocence and Experience" (New York: Oxford University Press, 1988), p. 276.
4. Phillips Brooks, "O Little Town of Bethlehem" (1868).